An Introduction to Computers
&
The Internet

For Children – ages 5 to 8 years.

by
Dennis E. Adonis

Stage 2

Inside Illustrations by: Kristen Fogarty

Published by:
Learning Tree Media
Great Britain

An Introduction to Computers and the Internet for Children Vol. 2: ages 5 - 8

Copyright © 2012 by Dennis Adonis

Learning Tree Publishers
West Sussex
Great Britain

Ordering Information:
For distribution details, please contact the publisher at:
info@learningtree.tk
www.learningtree.tk

First Printing, May 2012

An open letter to Parents

Dear Parents,

You would acknowledge that children are much smarter and technologically adapted than us when we would have been there age not so long ago.

Kids are almost overnight experts at reprogramming our smartphones, the game box and most computerize gadgets than even their parents, most of the times.

Until a few years ago a book of this nature would have been inconceivable, since most parents would have thought that teaching a 5, 6, 7, or 8 year old the fundamental aspects of computers, as practically unnecessary for a child of that age.

Ironically, today we have no other choice but to accept that a child without computer knowledge, even as small as five years old, can encounter serious difficulties to adapt to a computerize school environment later on, and by extension, find it difficult to reason effectively on such topics with children of his/ her age.

It is almost every good parents wish that there child receives nothing but the best that life has to offer, and in essence, the best education.

For every parent, the sooner their child can be drafted into understanding computer science, the better opportunities they may have for learning and adaptability down the road.

Therefore, in recognition of thousands of parents genuine desire to make their children computer educated from an early age, notable Guyanese Technology Author and Computer Software Engineer; Dennis E. Adonis has developed a simplified methodology aimed at teaching children to better understand computers.

Teaming up with Ms. Kristen Fogarty, one of the best children's book illustrators in the United States, he delivers information technology learning in a child friendly and simplified scenario that is certain to help your child understand all of the important aspects of computers.

This book is the second of a three-part series, and deals with the actual usage and internet benefits of a computer system. (Your Child must have Stage One of this book to better use this volume, which is State Two)

This strategy is essential, as it follows strongly on the foundation that was already laid out in Stage One of this book series, and actually prepares the child to effectively use a computer.

Your decision to get a copy of this book for your child was certainly an excellent choice, and open evidence that you care about their academic development and future survival in a technologically advancing generation.

Learning Tree Publishing

Parental advice

Please note that based upon a prior one month test of this book contents, there were subsequent scenarios where children reading this book have independently engage in the use of the internet with a great degree of effectiveness.

While this may be a good sign of their ability to adapt quickly, the Publishers and Author of this book wishes to advise parents against allowing children to engage in the independent or unsupervised use of the internet.

This book is intended to provide responsible education to children. Therefore, the Author or publisher would not hold themselves responsible for any child's action as a result of whatever they may have learnt from reading this book.

This is Mel. She had just finish having her dinner

She had learnt earlier about computer parts, and was now seated next to her Dad, Jim, who was teaching her.

Her Dad was settling himself at the computer desk, in the living room of the house.

She had learnt a few things about computers today, because her dad had earlier set up a new computer system in the home.

Mel was told that it was a desktop computer, which does the same thing as a laptop computer, iPad *(also called a slate),* and some smart phones.

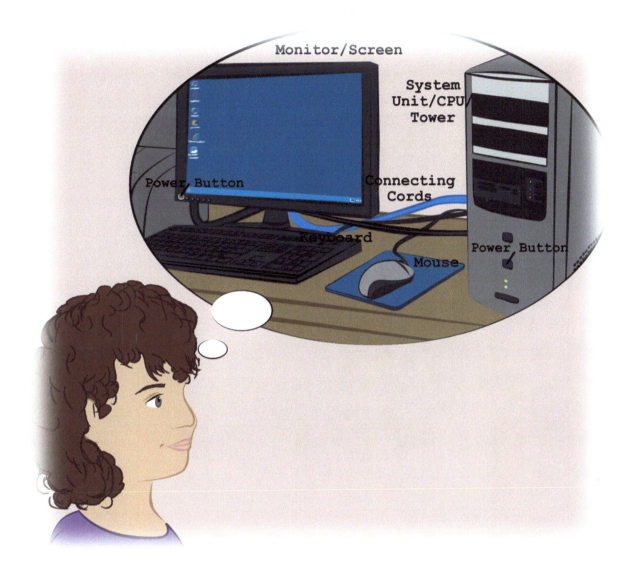

Mel had learnt that a desktop computer has many important parts.

There were many strange parts inside that makes' the computer work.

However it is mainly made up of a monitor (screen), a system unit (also called the CPU unit or the brain), a keyboard, a mouse, and connecting cords.

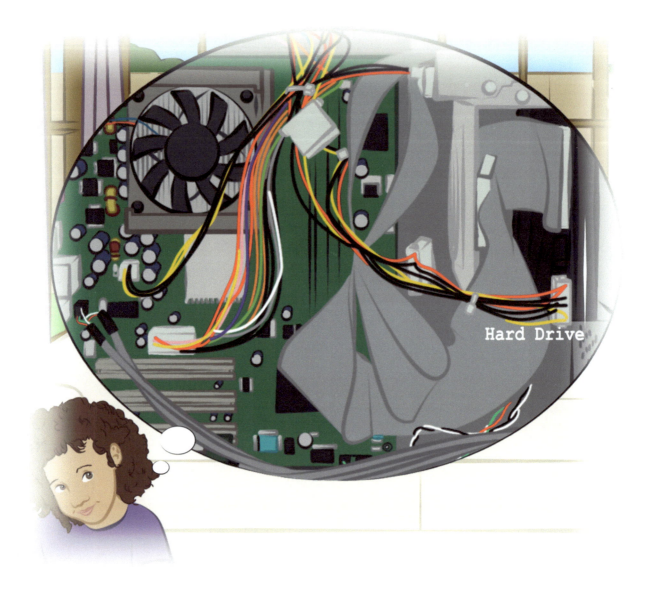

Hard Drive

She also learnt that all of the information of a computer is stored on a hard CD disk within the system unit.

The hard CD disk is known as the hard drive.

(1) Picture that is stored on computer hard drive

(2) Picture data flows through video cable

(3) Picture being printed

She was surprise to know that all of the pictures, videos and words of a computer are stored on the Hard Drive.

The Hard Drive sends the stored pictures and videos to the screen (monitor) through a special wire called the VGA or Video cable, so that people can see the information.

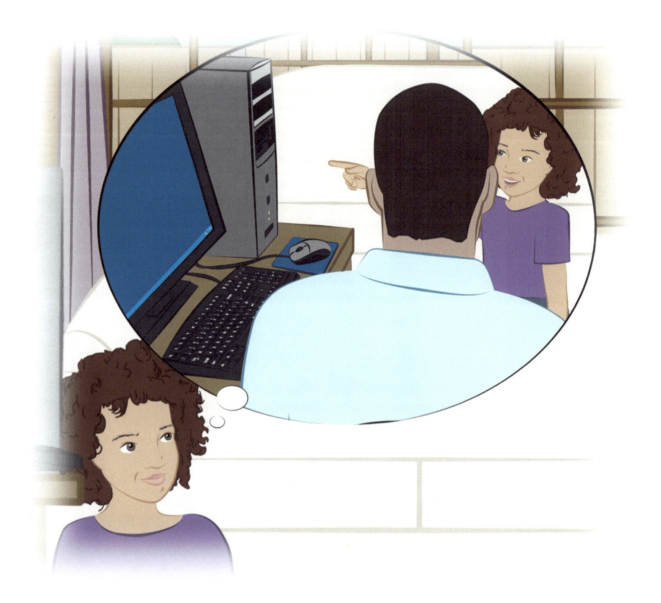

However, Mel was disappointed when she learnt that there were no pictures of sponge-bob or Dora on the computer.

Her Dad had told her that a computer brain (CPU unit and Hard Drive) only stores information that people had put into it.

She was told that in order to see or add more information to it, they can use other devices such a CD or Flash drive with information already on it.

However, the internet was sure to have all the pictures and information that she needs.

Mel was glad that the internet would certainly have lots of the information and pictures.

As such, she asked her Dad to get the pictures of Sponge-bob and Dora from the internet for her.

Now settled at the computer, her Dad reminded Mel that the computer would first have to be turned on.

He added that the <u>monitor</u> and the <u>system unit</u> would have to be turned on using their own power buttons which is usually at the front of them.

Remembering where the power buttons were, she smiled and pushed each button, when her Dad told her to do so.

Upon pressing each button, lights on the system unit *(CPU unit or brain tower)* starts blinking.

The screen *(or monitor)* also start to flicker on and off during the start-up process.

After a few seconds, the flickering stopped, and the computer screen
appeared with a background picture and some small objects.

Mel had learnt that the objects were called Icons, and the screen is
called, "the Desktop".
Icons are markers, or doorways to other things stored on the computer.

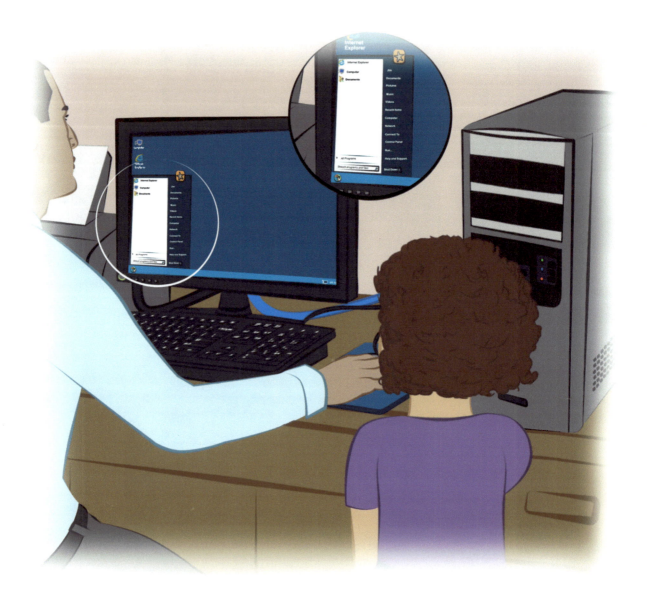

Her Dad explained that people can access things on the computer through these "shortcut Icons".

They can also get to the same items through the "Start Menu".

He then held the mouse and pointed it's <u>cursor</u> to a coloured icon at the lower left-bottom of the screen *(which is the start menu)* and clicked it.

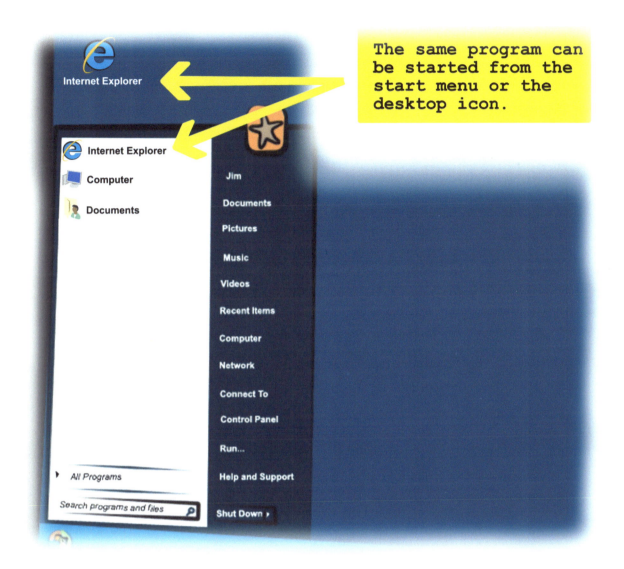

The same program can be started from the start menu or the desktop icon.

After clicking it, a menu quickly slides up with words and more icons.

Mel was told that these words on the slide-up menu are linked to the same things that the desktop icons are pointed to.

Therefore, she can click the words on the slide-up menu or the icons on the desktop to open programs, pictures, music and other things from the computer "Hard Drive" *(or brain)*.

However, Mel was told to click on a desktop icon instead, to connect to the internet, since it is easier and faster than using the <u>start menu</u>.

He then moved the mouse pointer from the start menu icon, and the slide-up items quickly disappeared.
The mouse was then focus on the "Internet Explorer" desktop icon.

Her Dad then exchanged seats with Mel and told her that he would show her how to connect to the internet.

Now sitting at the computer, Mel was confused with the desktop because there were lots of icons.

Each icon had a different shape, picture or symbol.

Her Dad then showed her all of the common icons that are usually used as shortcuts to the internet.

These were the Internet Explorer icon, Mozilla Firefox, Google Chrome, Apple Safari, and the Opera web browser icons.

Her Dad explained that each one of these internet programs (shortcuts) is called an "Internet Browser".

The word "browse" means "to look". As such they are programs that people uses to look through things on the internet.

He added that even though they have different names and icons, they all do the same thing; - which is to work as a browser to show information from the internet clearly.

If the computer does not have an internet browser, then you cannot see most things on the internet.

Mel's Dad then told her to click on one of the browser icons, and press the "Enter" key on the keyboard.

Mel did just that and a page popped up. But it showed an error message which said 'you are not connected to the internet".

Mel was unhappy and wondered why that had happened.

Her Dad explained that an internet icon on a computer does not mean that the computer has access to the internet.

He added that a special cable such as an internet active phone line is required.

If not, a network cable or wireless internet signal *(like what a cellular phone uses)* must be connected to the computer first.

Jim then took a special cable that was connected to a lighted box that was linked to the phone cord in the wall.

He told Mel that the box is called a "modem", and the special wire is called a 'network cable".

The network cable was then plugged behind the computer's CPU unit *(or system unit)*.

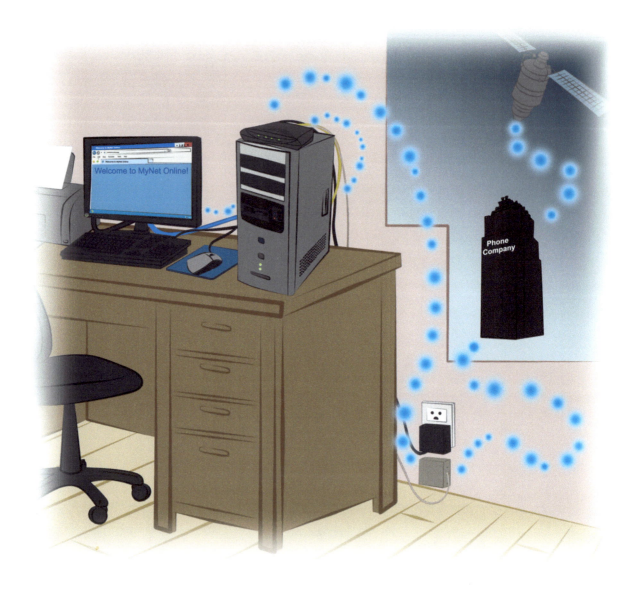

He told Mel that the modem collects information from the internet company and send it to the computer brain through the network cable.

The computer brain will then show the user the information from the internet, on the computer screen *(or monitor)*.

However, even though Mel had saw computers many times in the past, she had never actually had a chance to use one before.

Now that she was told how to use the computer, she did not know what is really meant by the "Internet" and what it is made of.

So, she questioned her dad about this.

Jim told Mel that the Internet is like a big global library, shopping mall and park that sits within a large imaginary village.

Within this village, millions of people and shops store information, exchange ideas, work, chat, sell things, and make friends, without actually having to be there.

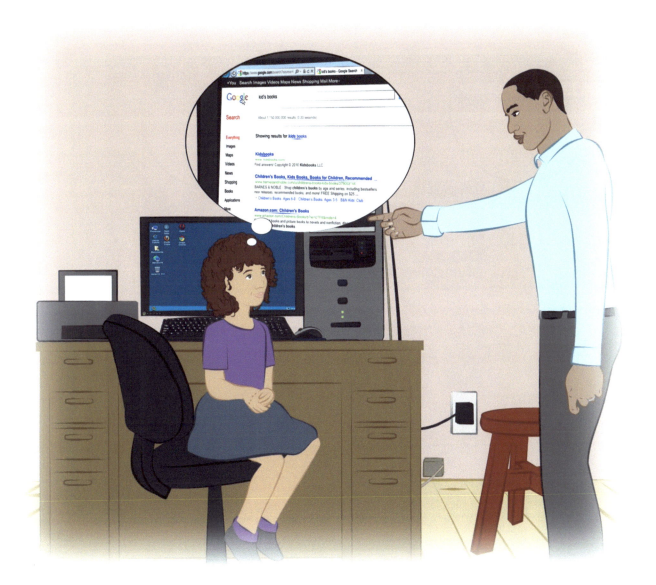

For example, you can search the internet for information on any topic, person or place.

When you are shown a list of search results, you can click one of the results and it will take you to a webpage about that topic.

You can also look for pictures, videos, books and maps on the internet.

Mel was excited, and asked her dad if the computer is now connected to the internet, to which he answered "yes".

At his nod, Mel clicked on one of the internet icons again, and this time, a webpage opens up on the computer screen.

She saw the words www.google.com in an open space at the top of the page. She learned that the long line is called the "address bar", while google.com is the address of the website that she is on.

The webpage had a big coloured word across the screen that said "Google" and a button marked "Search", with a long rectangular box above it.

Mel learnt that this is called a "search box", and is use to enter words of things that you wants to find on the internet.

Her dad then told her to type "spongebob pictures" in the search box, and click the "search" button, or press the "Enter" key on the keyboard.

After that was done, Mel saw the word "search results" along with a long list of numbered blue words and phrases below it.

Next to number one in the search results Mel saw *"dozens of spongebob pictures"*, then # 2: *Get spongebob pictures"*, followed by hundreds of others that listed something about spongebob.

Mel was confused and did not know what to do with the list before her.

Her dad then told her that; - the search results is like a library lists from which you can choose the webpage that looks like the information that you actually need.

When you see the desired item on the list, simply click on that item and it will take you to the actual webpage where the details are actually stored.

Mel was now able to understand that the website that first came up, (www.google.com) was a "search engine".

Search engines operates like thousands of library workers who quickly look for items that you may need, and then showing you a list of results on a page for you to choose from.

She also learnt that there are many other websites that works as a search engines, such as www.yahoo.com, and www.msn.com.

Now knowing that the search engine "Google" only lists links to other sites about spongebob, Mel clicked on a link in the search results.

A new colourful website opened up, and Mel could see lots of pictures and things about Spongebob on that page.

The new site is now showing itself as, *www.unitedspongebob.com*.

Mel was again confused about why the word *www.google.com* was now changed to *www.unitedspongebob.com*.

Her Dad then explained that each website has a separate web address. The web address tells Google *(and other search engines)* and the computer, where the information that you want is located.

This operates in the same way as your address, where someone can only find you if they know where you are located.

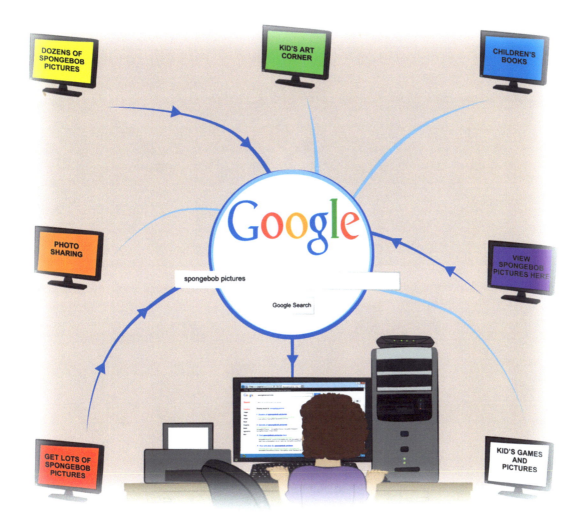

He added that in the same way, Google search must have an address location for the results so that the computer will take you to that web address when you click on a link in the search results.

The "www" stands for "World Wide Web". So when you type **www.**, the computer immediately knows that the address that you are looking for is on the Internet, and not the computer brain itself.

So it will go to the World Wide Web, first.

Having learnt this, Mel soon began to search for lots of other things such as children's games, Dora the explorer, and Spiderman, for almost two hours.

She then remembers her friends talking about Email, Facebook, Myspace and internet chatting in school.

Being curious, she asked her dad to explain what they are and their uses.

Notice to Parents

This section of the book deals with social networking and the ability to communicate with other people over the internet.

Children studying this information can subsequently adapt to the use of email, in addition to websites (not intended for children under 13) such as Facebook, Twitter, Myspace and similar social websites unknowing to parents.

Therefore, parents should be mindful about introducing their children to social networking, as it often becomes habitual and can be a child safety problem if not effectively policed by a guardian.

If you are concerned about this, you may want to consider removing the remaining pages *(from page # 36 onwards)* of this book or simply restrict their reading beyond this point.

This section of this book is more understandable to children from age 7 and above, even though the entire lesson itself can be taught to children from ages five upward.

However, teaching them the following lesson is a parent's individual choice, subject to the various advantages and disadvantages of opening-up social networking and email communication knowledge to your child.

Mel's Dad told her that an email is a letter or message sent by one person to another person's email address *(personal internet address)* using a computer.

It works just like a text message from one cell phone to the other.

However, the sender must have an email address and the receiver must have an email address that is known to each other, in order to chat.

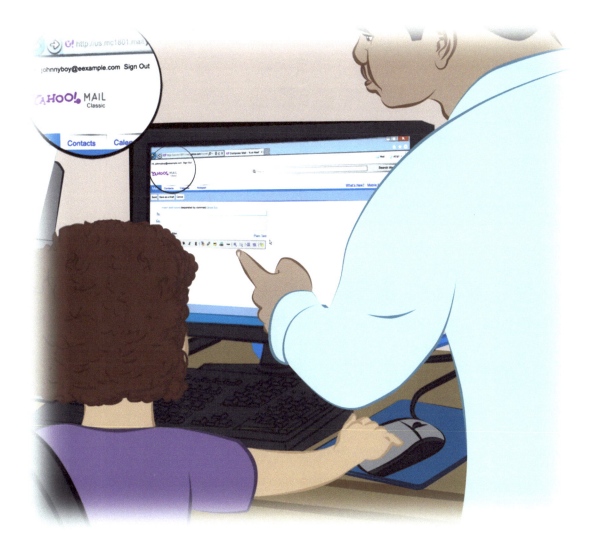

To send an email message, the sender must have an internet email address, which looks something like this: dennisadonis@example.com

This means "dennisadonis" is the sender's username *(like a phone number).*

The @ sign means "at", while "example.com" is the company at which "dennisadonis" receives his email messages on the internet.

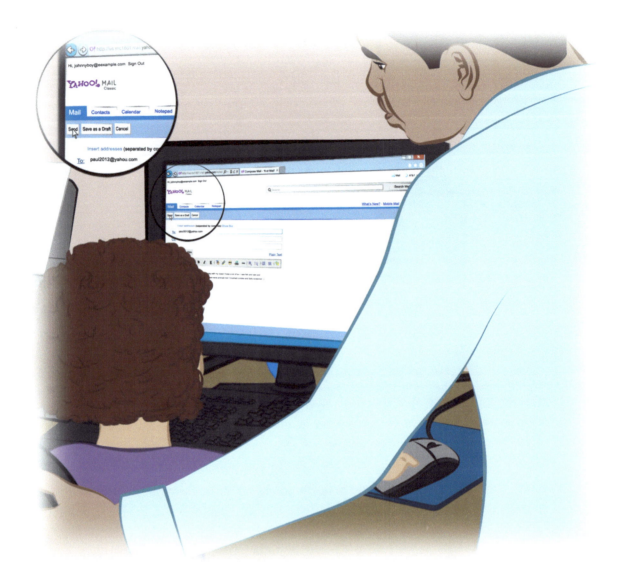

Let's say Dennis wants to send an email message to his friend Paul, whose email address is: paul2012@example.com.

He would first have to sign into his dennisadonis@example.com email, and then type the messages from his address in order to send it to Paul's email address.

Paul can then receive Dennis message wherever in the world he may be.

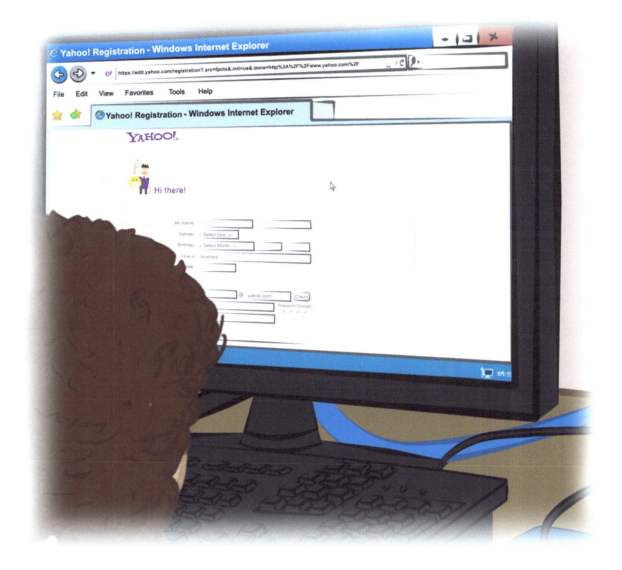

To get a parents-managed email address, you can ask your mom or dad to use the computer browser, and go to either:

1 – http://mail.yahoo.com
2 – www.gmail.com, or
3 – www.hotmail.com

And click on the 'Sign up" button, to help set up your email address.

Once you have an email address you will now be able to chat with other people (like grown-ups do on Facebook).

You will also be able to join children-safe social websites like; -

(1) www.skid-e-kids.com
(2) http://disney.go.com/create
(3) www.whatswhat.me

Mel was excited about the many good things you can do on the internet, and decided to take some time to visit many websites.

However her dad told Mel that the internet also has many bad things that can put kids and their family in danger.

Mel was very surprised, and wondered aloud what some of the bad things can be.

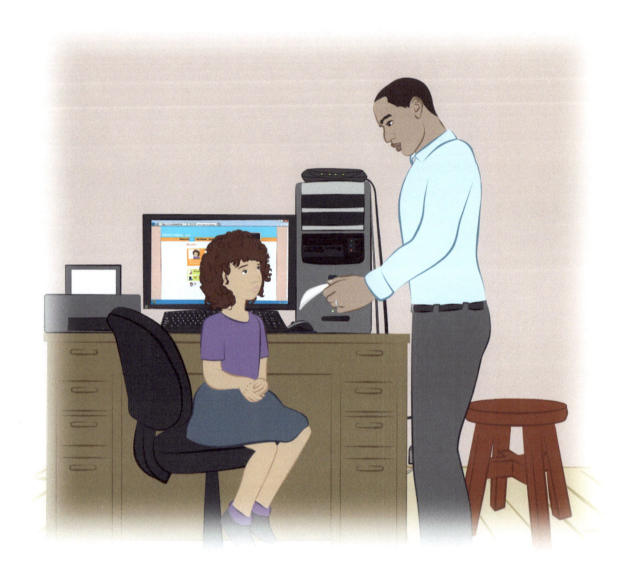

Her dad said that there are many bad things. But if you obey some basic rules, then it should be ok.

He then gave her a paper listing a series of rules and things she should be careful about on the World Wide Web.

Mel took the paper, and read through a long list of things she should observe whenever she is using the internet.

Internet Safety Rules for children

- Never turn on the computer and connect to the internet without your parents' approval.

- Do not use your friend's computer or an internet café without your parents' approval.

- Do not sign up for something online if your parents did not tell you to do so.

- Do not give your email address to people without your parents' consent.

- Do not reply to email addresses that you don't know

- Do not visit websites that your parents have not approved.

- Do not download anything, including things saying "you won" or "games".

- Never tell anyone on the internet where you live.

- Do not give anyone online information about yourself, parents, family and their jobs.

- Never look at pictures and things that are intended for adults online.

- You are a kid; avoid chatting online with people that your parents did not approve.

- Do not share pictures of yourself, your family or your home with other people online.

- Never use a webcam unless your parents told you to do so in their presence.

- Do not join social websites that is not intended for people above your age group

- Do not use false information to access websites not intended for your age group.

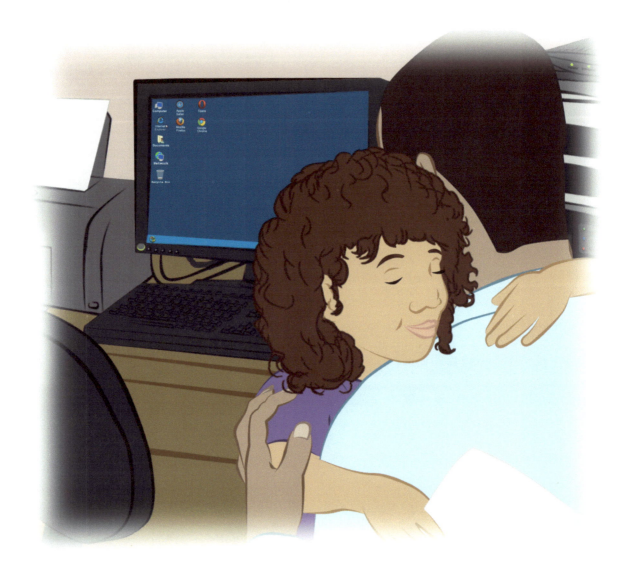

After reading the rules, Mel felt glad that her Dad had guided her about the things she should not do when using the internet.

Mel told her Dad that she would always obey those rules because she cares about herself and her family's safety.

She thanked her Dad for teaching her about computers and the internet.

She had wanted to use the computer again, but it was now 8pm, and her eyes began to feel very sleepy.

With sleepy eyes, she told Dad that she was tired and is going off to bed.

Mel then told her dad "good night", rubbed her sleepy eyes and quickly went off to bed.

In the meantime, her Dad took the mouse and select the start button at the bottom left of the screen.

He then clicked the word that said "shut down" from the slide up menu.

The computer screen soon began to flicker, and was off a few seconds later. It will remain off until Mel's Dad puts it on again tomorrow.

The End

About the Author

Dennis E. Adonis is a prominent Guyanese Computer Software Engineer, Musician, Educational Author and Folk Novelist.

As of May 2012, he had written over a dozen books, half of which are based on Computer Science, including four children books in the same spirit as this one.

Mr. Adonis, himself a father of five adorable children, is known to be an excellent mentor and educator as it relates to helping children to understand the fundamental aspects of Information Technology regardless of their age grouping.

He had served as a mentor on many Children's computer teaching projects in the Caribbean and Europe, and had headed two *Unicef* assisted-projects aimed at teaching computers to children in his home country Guyana between 2005 and 2006.

His educational background in a variety of fields has also allowed him to be avail as a consultant for various entities over the years, but mostly as a Computer Security Software Engineer.

Outside of his work as an outstanding Author, he is currently a Contributing writer on Information Technology at Yahoo.com, and an *Adjunct* Curriculum Developer in Information Technology at Warnborough College, in England.

To interact with the Author, visit his Official Website at: **www.dennisadonis.net**

Author's Bio compiled by: Ms. Deon Brown
Learning Tree Publishing – Great Britain.

www.ingramcontent.com/pod-product-compliance
Lightning Source LLC
Chambersburg PA
CBHW041423050326
40689CB00002B/625